T0130391

AuthorHouse™
1663 Liberty Drive
Bloomington, IN 47403
www.authorhouse.com
Phone: 833-262-8899

Because of the dynamic nature of the Internet, any web addresses or links contained in this book may have changed since publication and may no longer be valid. The views expressed in this work are solely those of the author and do not necessarily reflect the views of the publisher, and the publisher hereby disclaims any responsibility for them.

Any people depicted in stock imagery provided by Getty Images are models, and such images are being used for illustrative purposes only. Certain stock imagery © Getty Images.

This book is printed on acid-free paper.

ISBN: 978-1-6655-5164-9 (sc)
ISBN: 978-1-6655-5163-2 (e)

Library of Congress Control Number: 2022902857

Print information available on the last page.

Published by AuthorHouse 02/09/2022

authorHOUSE®

YOU CAN DO ANYTHING

1

"Strike three!" the umpire shouted. Xavier stood on the pitcher's mound with a big smile on his face.

"Let's go Xavier! Go Tigers!" the crowd roared.

His opponent lowered his bat and wandered away from home plate. After him, Xavier struck out two more players, the inning ended, and the Tigers won the game. Xavier's teammates ran onto the field and tackled him on the mound, slapping his back and giving him high fives.

"Way to go, Xavier!" they shouted.

After the game, the Tigers celebrated with waffle cones at Molly's Place. They took up half the parlor, and made half the noise too.

Some players from the other team, The Hurricanes, walked into Molly's to get some ice cream. Xavier and a few of his teammates walked up to them with a smile, "Great game! You guys played really well."

The boy in the center frowned, "You guys got lucky," he said.

"Your pitcher cheated. Boys like you aren't supposed to be playing baseball anyways. I don't even know how you got on your team."

"Boys like me?" Xavier asked.

"Black boys," the one in the center responded, "You guys aren't good at anything."

Before Xavier could respond, the three boys walked away, laughing and poking fun at him. He thought about what they said for the rest of the day, and by the time he got home, his mother noticed how quiet he'd been.

"What's wrong, sweetheart?"

Xavier took off his cap and threw it on the couch, shrugging his shoulders, "Some of The Hurricanes were at Molly's and they said that I don't belong on the team. That because I'm black, it means I don't belong with the other Tigers."

His mother sighed and sat on the couch next to him, pulling him into her side, "I'm sorry that happened. It wasn't kind of them to say those things."

"Well, were they right?" Xavier asked, "Do I not belong?"

"Of course you do. Xavier, boys like that, they are taught how to hate. To say and believe mean, dishonest things about people who are different from them. It's not right, but unfortunately, it happens really often. The best we can do is ignore them, and continue to do what we love. You're a good baseball player, Xavier, don't ever let anyone take that away from you. You might be different, yes, but that doesn't mean that you belong any less. In fact, it makes you all the more special. Believe in yourself, love. When you do, you can do anything."

Xavier held onto his mother's words. He took them with him to every tryout, game, and practice. As he grew up, he met more people that chose not to believe in him because of his skin color. People doubted him because he was different, but when that happened, he thought about what his mother said, and that kept him from listening to those unkind words. It kept him from being afraid.

Years later, Xavier became a pitcher for his high school team, The Pirates. He continued to work hard, and it showed in his games. He struck out lots of other players, and helped his team win a lot of games.

Xavier's Senior year, The Pirates won his city's baseball championship. To celebrate, they all went out to Molly's Place.

"Xavier Thomas?" a voice called. Xavier turned from his table to see a man in a grey suit standing above him.

"Yes, how can I help you?"

"I am recruiting for the Texas University Longhorns baseball team."

"The best team in the country," Xavier said.

The man smiled, "That we are. Listen, now that you are a senior, I'm sure you've started looking at colleges where you can continue to play, and I'd like for you to consider us."

"Really?"

"You are quite talented, Xavier. It's been a long time since we've been able to find a player like you."

The man reached into his coat pocket and pulled out a card, "Give me a call when you're ready to start talking scholarships."

Xavier grinned and shook the man's hand, "I will."

Xavier's mother had come to the game, like she did all of them, but she wasn't in the mood for ice cream so she went home right after it ended. He was so excited to tell her the news that he left his waffle cone melting on the table, and ran several blocks all the way home.

He burst in the door to find his mother reading on the couch. "What in the world?" she said with a smile, "What are you so excited about?"

"The Texas Longhorns! The best team in the whole country, they want me to play for them!"

His mother got up from the couch and wrapped Xavier in a hug. "I knew you could do it."

"Because of you," he replied.

"Just like I told you," she said, "Believe in yourself, love."

"When you do, you can do anything." Xavier finished.

Printed in the United States
by Baker & Taylor Publisher Services